MY FAMILY

Collected Memories

MARY BETH SAMMONS

BARNES & NOBLE BOOKS

NEW YORK

Book design by Lundquist Design, New York

ISBN 0-7607-6721-1

Printed and bound in the United States of America

10 9 8 7 6 5 4 3 2 1

Table of Contents

Introduction

Welcome. This book is a book about you and your family. It's an interactive journal written for you and your family, by you. The twist is that this book takes you on a journey backward, through the lives of your family and ancestors, so that when you better understand their stories and struggles to live abundantly, you and your family members will gain clearer insight, direction, and courage to uncover the real you and your family members at work, at home, and wherever your journeys are destined to take all of you.

My Family: Collected Memories is a place for you to begin to write the exciting narrative of your family history and in the process gain insights into how those people, memories, and events have shaped all of you. This journal also will help you begin shaping your story for those who will carry on in your path.

More often than not, we discover who we are and what we love through revelations found in the small, simple, and common patterns that have been woven together in the threads of joy and sorrow by the generations before us. Once you appreciate this larger tapestry, it enriches the pattern of your own life. It also unravels some of the mystery surrounding who you really are in your search for meaning and identity. We hope that the capacity for wonder, beauty, and meeting challenges forged by your family members will provide a compass for you and the next generation.

Family stories are tales about people, places, and events related to the members of our immediate family or our ancestors, and even close friends who have become extended family. Let this memory journal be a starting point—a door to writing and sharing the unique qualities of your family's life.

How to Use This Book

There is a lot of material here. Feel free to spend time in the chapters that most interest you. The book starts by asking you to step backward to explore how the characteristics of your ancestors influenced you today. What were your parents' achievements? What were their expectations for you? Who are the people you would count on to listen, give advice, inspire, and guide you? How did they end up doing the work they did? As you start filling out the pages of this book, you will see how your family members experienced different areas of their life, from leisure and play to careers, romance, spirituality, and family. Consider these nuggets of wisdom and the people who lived them as life advisors. What do your answers to the questions about your family tell you about yourself?

How to Uncover the Truth

Discovering all the answers to these questions about family may not always be easy, especially since some of your relatives are no longer here to help you in the exploration. But, there are other ways to uncover, discover, and recover the mysterious parts of your family history and get reacquainted and reconnected with their lives. Each chapter offers questions and wisdom-filled quotations to help inspire greater understanding and insight.

Where to Begin the Search

Interview Elders

The easiest and most effective way to uncover family stories is to ask questions. Interviewing a family elder, or perhaps a close friend of the family, can help you collect family stories. You may even consider handing this book over to the family member or friend for a short period to fill in some of the answers on his or her own. Make a mental or written list of topics that might generate some questions to ask older relatives and family friends. Although short-term memory may sometimes be limited in the oldest of relatives, long-term memory may often be very much intact. You need to help the teller journey back in time to retrieve these treasures.

Interview Other Family Members

Don't overlook the sibling or cousin who may have collected stories of family, recipes, photographs, favorite quotes, and snippets of wisdom from family members—young and old.

Jog Your Memory with Other Sources of Information

In some cases, you may not be able to interview the source for information. But information and events can be revealed in other ways, if you are creative and are enthusiastic about taking on the role of reporter. Photographs, letters or cards, yearbooks, and other memorabilia can all serve to reveal information about ancestors and bring back those memories that have been pushed to the back of your brain. If you can get access to the belongings left behind by ancestors and living relatives, some places to look for answers include:

Autograph books
Bibles
Books (Check for inscriptions in them.)
Certificates (from schools or jobs)
Church records
Cookbooks
Diaries and daybooks
Family trees
Photo albums

Important papers (wills, titles, and deeds)
Jewelry (such as pins, ID bracelets, charm bracelets, lockets, or anything else
    that may have an inscription or indicate membership in an organization)
Letters
Newspaper clippings
Pictures (Don't forget to look at the backs.)
Résumés
School papers
Scrapbooks
Sewing samplers, quilts, and other handmade items
Trunks and chests
Yearbooks

Now It Is Time to Get Started . . .

The purpose of this book, which is really about you—your family history, your childhood memories, funny incidents, and meaningful traditions in your life—is to help you and the generations that will follow you to understand their lives better. So, from their hearts to yours, it is time to tell your family story.

"The family is one of nature's masterpieces."

—George Santayana

CHAPTER ONE

Portraits: Creating Your Family Tree

*"With all beings and all things
we shall be as relatives."*

— Sioux Indian proverb

Portraits: Creating Your Family Tree

Begin your journal autobiography by mapping the family tree of your ancestors, those who have come before you and the next generation who already are making their mark in the world. This will give you a chronological road map and the skeleton of your story, which is a good place to begin. Don't worry about the exact dates of birth or death, but concentrate on sketching down a few personal details about each family member. Think about stories you have heard about them, nicknames, and the unique attributes that made each and every one of them special. The best starting point: yourself.

Me
Date of Birth:

Occupation(s):

Defining Life Moments:

1.

2.

3.

Siblings
Date of Birth:

1.

2.

3.

Mother
Date of Birth:

Occupation(s):

Defining Life Moments:

Father
Date of Birth:

Occupation(s):

Defining Life Moments:

Mother's side of the family continues on page 3

Father's side of the family continues on page 6

Mother's Side of Family
(continued from page 2)

Aunts/Uncles
Date of Birth:
Sibling 1:
Sibling 2:
Sibling 3:

Occupation(s):
Sibling 1:
Sibling 2:
Sibling 3:

Defining Life Moments:

Sibling 1:

Sibling 2:

Sibling 3:

Maternal Grandmother
Date of Birth:

Occupation(s):

Defining Life Moments:

1.

2.

3.

*Maternal grandmother's side of the family
continues on page 4*

Maternal Grandfather
Date of Birth:

Occupation(s):

Defining Life Moments:

1.

2.

3.

*Maternal grandfather's side of the family
continues on page 5*

Mother's Side of Family
Maternal Grandmother's Side
(continued from page 3)

Great Aunts/Uncles
Date of Birth:
Sibling 1:

Sibling 2:

Sibling 3:

Occupation(s):
Sibling 1:

Sibling 2:

Sibling 3:

Defining Life Moments:
Sibling 1:

Sibling 2:

Sibling 3:

Maternal Great-Grandmother #1
Date of Birth:

Occupation(s):

Defining Life Moments:
1.

2.

Maternal Great-Grandfather #1
Date of Birth:

Occupation(s):

Defining Life Moments:
1.

2.

Mother's Side of Family
Maternal Grandfather's Side
(continued from page 3)

Great-Aunts/-Uncles
Date of Birth:
Sibling 1:

Sibling 2:

Sibling 3:

Occupation(s):
Sibling 1:

Sibling 2:

Sibling 3:

Defining Life Moments
Sibling 1:

Sibling 2:

Sibling 3:

Maternal Great-Grandmother #2
Date of Birth:

Occupation(s):

Defining Life Moments:
1.

2.

Maternal Great-Grandfather #2
Date of Birth:

Occupation(s):

Defining Life Moments:
1.

2.

Father's Side of Family
(continued from page 2)

Aunts/Uncles
Date of birth:
Sibling 1:

Sibling 2:

Sibling 3:

Occupation(s):
Sibling 1:

Sibling 2:

Sibling 3:

Defining Life Moments:
Sibling 1:

Sibling 2:

Sibling 3:

Paternal Grandmother
Date of Birth:

Occupation(s):

Defining Life Moments:
1.

2.

3.

*Paternal grandmother's side of the family
continues on page 7*

Paternal Grandfather
Date of Birth:

Occupation(s):

Defining Life Moments:
1.

2.

3.

*Paternal grandfather's side of the family
continues on page 8*

Father's Side of Family
Paternal Grandmother's Side
(continued from page 6)

Great-Aunts/-Uncles
Date of Birth:
Sibling 1:

Sibling 2:

Sibling 3:

Occupation(s):
Sibling 1:

Sibling 2:

Sibling 3:

Defining Life Moments:
Sibling 1:

Sibling 2:

Sibling 3:

Paternal Great-Grandmother #1
Date of Birth:

Occupation(s):

Defining Life Moments:
1.

2.

Paternal Great-Grandfather #1
Date of Birth:

Occupation(s):

Defining Life Moments:
1.

2.

Father's Side of Family
Paternal Grandfather's Side
(continued from page 6)

Great-Aunts/-Uncles
Date of Birth:
Sibling 1:

Sibling 2:

Sibling 3:

Occupation(s):
Sibling 1:

Sibling 2:

Sibling 3:

Defining Life Moments:
Sibling 1:

Sibling 2:

Sibling 3:

Paternal Great-Grandmother #2
Date of Birth:

Occupation(s):

Defining Life Moments:
1.

2.

Paternal Great-Grandfather #2
Date of Birth:

Occupation(s):

Defining Life Moments:
1.

2.

My Spouse/Significant Other

Date of Birth:

Occupation(s):

Defining Life Moments:
1.

2.

3.

My Spouse/Significant Other's Family
Parents:

Grandparents:

Siblings:

Nieces and Nephews:

My Children

Names/Ages:

Dates of Birth:

Occupation(s)/School Years:

Defining Life Moments:

My Grandchildren

Names/Ages:

Dates of Birth:

Occupation(s)/School Years:

Defining Life Moments:

"The linking of generations, the historical lineage of family, the sharing of love . . . give purpose to life."

—George Landberg

My Siblings' Spouses

Sibling 1:

Sibling 2:

Sibling 3:

My Siblings' Children

Nieces and Nephews

Sibling 1:

Sibling 2:

Sibling 3:

Cousin Profile
Maternal Side

First Cousins:

Cousins' Children:

Second Cousins:

Cousins' Children:

Cousin Profile
Paternal Side

First Cousins:

Cousins' Children:

Second Cousins:

Cousins' Children:

What do you know about your great-great-grandparents?
Maternal Side

_____

_____

_____

_____

_____

_____

_____

_____

_____

_____

Paternal Side

_____

_____

_____

_____

_____

_____

_____

_____

_____

_____

_____

_____

Have you or your spouse been married more than once?

_____

_____

_____

_____

_____

_____

_____

_____

_____

_____

_____

Do you have additional family members? Stepchildren?

_____

_____

_____

_____

_____

_____

_____

_____

_____

_____

_____

_____

Don't overlook doing a family tree if you, your children, or any of your family members are adopted or are stepchildren and family through divorce or other extenuating circumstances. You can enjoy tracing the history of whomever you consider family.

Adopted Families

In most states, adoption records are sealed and can be opened only for reasons that the courts determine are serious enough to warrant doing so. However, you can create a family tree from information you or your parents know about ancestors, and you can also create a family tree for the family who has adopted you.

Your Biological Parents
Mother

Name (if you know it):

Native Country and Town of Birthplace:

Defining Moments:

Occupation(s):

Maternal Grandparents' Names (both sides of the family):

Mother's Siblings:

Any other details you know about mother's side of family:

Your Biological Parents
Father

Name (if you know it):

Native Country and Town of Birthplace:

Defining Moments:

Occupation(s):

Paternal Grandparents' Names (both sides of family):

Father's Siblings:

Any other details you know about your father's side of the family:

Stepfamilies

Stepmother's Name: _____

Birthplace: _____

Defining Moments: _____

Grandparents' Names (both sides): _____

Siblings: _____

Stepmother's Children (your stepbrothers and stepsisters): _____

_____

Any other details you know about your stepmother's side of the family: _____

_____

_____

_____

Stepfather's Name: _____

Birthplace: _____

Defining Moments: _____

Grandparents' Names (both sides): _____

Siblings: _____

Stepfather's Children (your stepbrothers and stepsisters): _____

_____

Any other details you know about your stepfather's side of the family: _____

_____

_____

_____

Do you have any stepsisters?

_____
_____
_____
_____
_____
_____
_____
_____
_____
_____
_____

Do you have any stepbrothers?

_____
_____
_____
_____
_____
_____
_____
_____
_____
_____
_____
_____

Do you have half sisters? Did you grow up with them?

_____

_____

_____

_____

_____

_____

_____

_____

_____

_____

Do you have half brothers? Are you very close to any of them?_____

_____

_____

_____

_____

_____

_____

_____

_____

_____

_____

_____

Friends as Family

Best Family Friends: _____

_____

_____

_____

_____

Parents' Best Friends: _____

_____

_____

_____

_____

Mom's Friends: _____

_____

_____

_____

Dad's Friends: _____

_____

_____

_____

_____

Friends of Whole Family: _____

_____

_____

_____

_____

_____

"When you start talking about family, about lineage, about ancestry, you are talking about every person on earth."

—Alex Haley

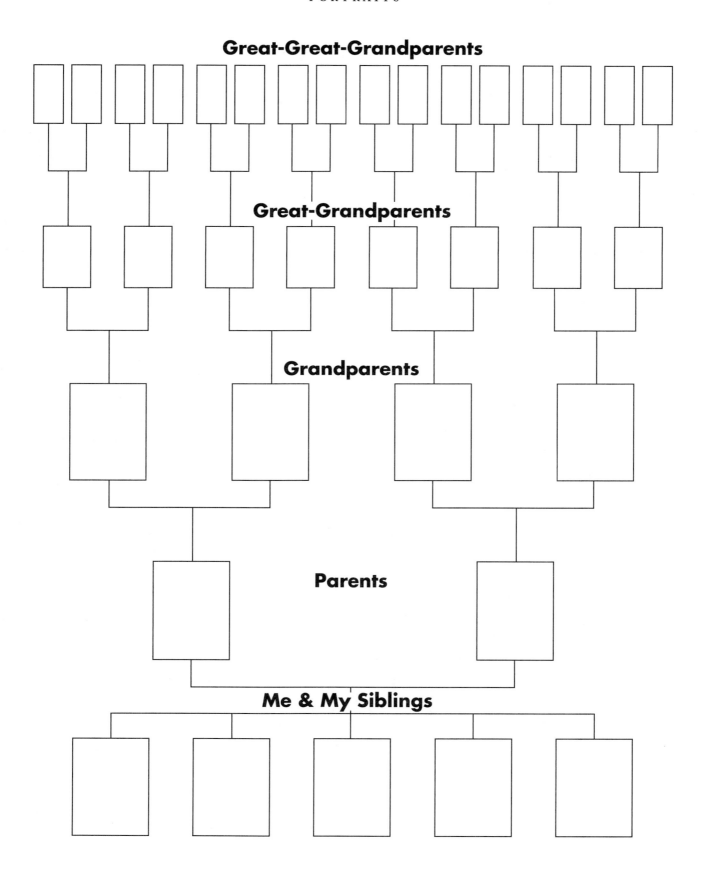

Great-Great-Grandparents

Great-Grandparents

Grandparents

Parents

Me & My Siblings

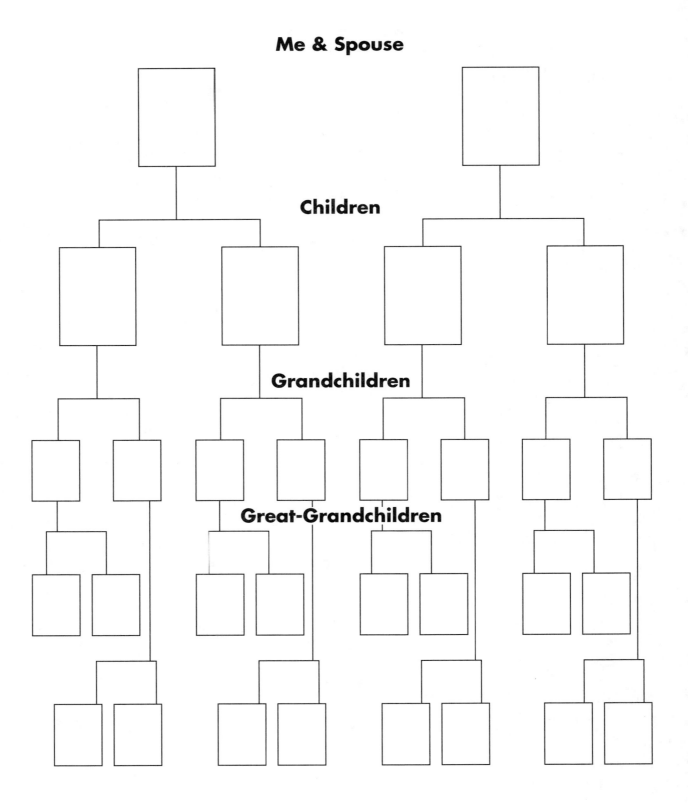

Me & Spouse

Children

Grandchildren

Great-Grandchildren

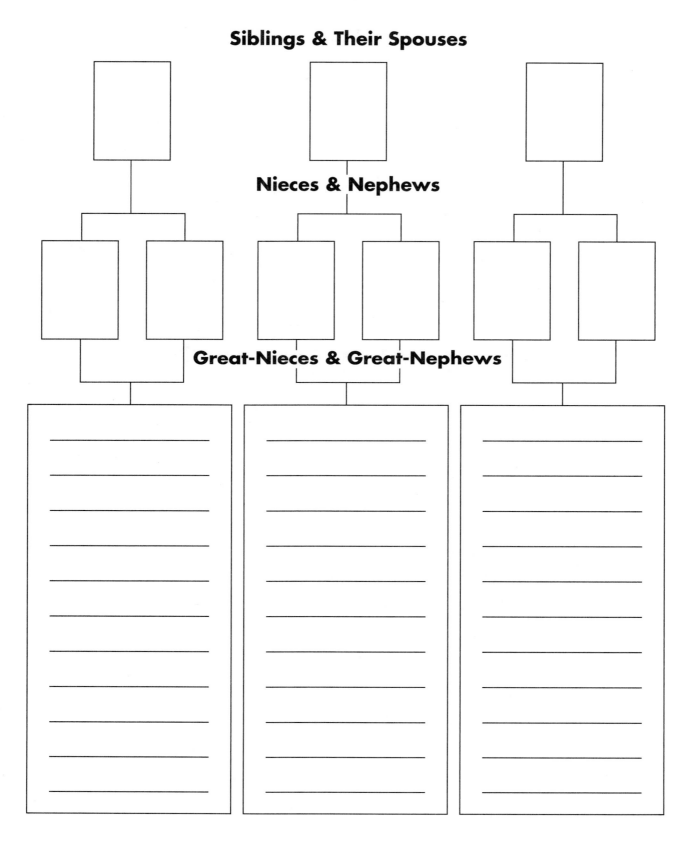

Siblings & Their Spouses

Nieces & Nephews

Great-Nieces & Great-Nephews

Behind the Name

"It is indeed a desirable thing to be well descended, but the glory belongs to our ancestors."

—*Plutarch*

Behind the Name

You are linked to your past by your family name, which has been in existence for many years, perhaps hundreds or thousands of years. Understanding the origins of your family surname helps give insights into the people who have come before you and the legacy you are passing on to your own family.

What do you know about your family surname? What is its origin? Was it taken from the Bible? Was it the name of a village? An occupation? An ancient landmark? Does your name mean something in another language?

_____

_____

_____

_____

_____

_____

_____

_____

Who were your ancestors who proudly bore this fine family name? Describe some of the notable ones you remember here.

_____

_____

_____

_____

_____

_____

_____

_____

Around the World

Can you trace your family name to a country, particular part of the world, or trade your ancestors practiced?

_____
_____
_____
_____
_____
_____
_____
_____
_____
_____

Is there a family emblem or coat of arms? A definition of what your family name means in another language?

_____
_____
_____
_____
_____
_____
_____
_____
_____
_____
_____
_____
_____
_____

Changing or modifying a family name was a common practice for immigrants when they arrived in the United States. Some had their names changed; others changed their names to more easily assimilate in the American culture. Was your family's original surname changed? What was the original name?

_____

_____

_____

_____

_____

_____

_____

_____

_____

Do any of your modern-day relatives continue to use the original name, or have any of them used the family surname as a first name for their children?

_____

_____

_____

_____

_____

_____

_____

_____

_____

_____

_____

Coming to America

When did the first family members come to America? Where did they come from? How did they get here? Are any family members still abroad?

_____

_____

_____

_____

_____

_____

_____

_____

_____

_____

Where did your ancestors first land? Where did they settle? Where did they move?

_____

_____

_____

_____

_____

_____

_____

_____

_____

_____

_____

What generation of American are you, and what countries do you have in your bloodline?

_____

_____

_____

_____

_____

_____

_____

_____

_____

_____

What nationalities are you? What physical traits do you display that are representative of that ancestry?

_____

_____

_____

_____

_____

_____

_____

_____

_____

_____

If your family's name was changed, do you not know the original name?

_____
_____
_____
_____
_____
_____
_____
_____
_____
_____
_____
_____

Were your ancestors separated from other family members? Are you able to search for lost relatives?

_____
_____
_____
_____
_____
_____
_____
_____
_____
_____
_____
_____

"The only rock I know that stays steady, the only institution I know that works is the family."

—Lee Iacocca

Maiden Voyages

What are your mother's, grandmother's, and great-grandmother's maiden names (including your dad's side too)?

_____

_____

_____

_____

_____

_____

_____

_____

_____

_____

_____

Do you know what those names mean or what significance they have?

_____

_____

_____

_____

_____

_____

_____

_____

_____

_____

Were you named after a certain relative, a famous person, or someone else? Who gave you your name and why? Or, is there any other significance to your naming?

_____

_____

_____

_____

_____

_____

_____

_____

_____

_____

Is there a naming tradition in your family, such as always giving the firstborn son the name of his paternal grandfather?

_____

_____

_____

_____

_____

_____

_____

_____

_____

"*Other things may change us, but we start and end with the family.*"

—Anthony Brandt

What is the full name of your mom? Her siblings? Her parents? Does your full name include any nicknames you have or may have had in the past?

_____

_____

_____

_____

_____

_____

_____

_____

_____

_____

_____

Do any of your relatives or ancestors have particularly distinctive names? Do you know what the significance of those names is, or why they were chosen?

_____

_____

_____

_____

_____

_____

_____

_____

_____

_____

_____

Are there first names or variations of names that have been carried on for generations?

_____

_____

_____

_____

_____

_____

_____

_____

_____

_____

_____

What are some of your family members' or ancestors' nicknames? What do they stand for? Do other people tend to assume or create nicknames from your family surname, and if so what are they?

_____

_____

_____

_____

_____

_____

_____

_____

_____

Mirror, Mirror

If you were named for someone else, what characteristics do family members tell you that you share with your namesake?

_____

_____

_____

_____

_____

_____

_____

_____

_____

_____

Were any of your siblings named for family members and, if so, what traits do they share with the relatives they were named for?

_____

_____

_____

_____

_____

_____

_____

_____

_____

What are your aunts' and uncles' names and nicknames? Do they have any special significance?

_____

_____

_____

_____

_____

_____

_____

_____

_____

_____

_____

Did your aunts and uncles pass any of the family names on to their children?

_____

_____

_____

_____

_____

_____

_____

_____

_____

_____

Are there any family members, you and your parents gave nicknames to or assigned traits to? Funny names? What did they mean? Did you tell the person?

_____

_____

_____

_____

_____

_____

_____

_____

_____

_____

_____

_____

Do you have any family members who have brought your family name fame? If so, who, and how are they famous?

_____

_____

_____

_____

_____

_____

_____

_____

_____

_____

Kid Stuff

How did you choose the names for your children? What do they mean, and what significance, if any, does that play in your family history?

_____

_____

_____

_____

_____

_____

_____

_____

_____

_____

_____

_____

What nicknames do you have for your children, if any?

_____

_____

_____

_____

_____

_____

_____

_____

_____

_____

_____

How were the names of your grandchildren chosen?

_____

_____

_____

_____

_____

_____

_____

_____

_____

_____

_____

Were any of your grandchildren or great-nieces and great-nephews named for you or other members of your family?

_____

_____

_____

_____

_____

_____

_____

_____

_____

_____

_____

_____

"Proper names are poetry in the raw.
Like all poetry they are untranslatable."

—W. H. Auden

A Friend Indeed

What are the names of the friends who have earned an honorary role as "family"? Do you call them "Aunt" or "Uncle"?

_____

_____

_____

_____

_____

_____

_____

_____

_____

Are there younger members of their families that you now call cousins? What are their names and nicknames?

_____

_____

_____

_____

_____

_____

_____

_____

_____

_____

_____

Do any of your cousins share names handed down from ancestors? Do you have an unusual number of some names in your family? Or any Seniors, Juniors, and the III's?

_____

_____

_____

_____

_____

_____

_____

_____

_____

_____

_____

_____

Have you ever looked up the meanings of your names and if so what do they mean?

_____

_____

_____

_____

_____

_____

_____

_____

_____

_____

What is your spouse or significant other's surname? Did his or her family come from a particular part of the world?

_____
_____
_____
_____
_____
_____
_____
_____
_____
_____
_____

Where? Does the name have any special meaning?

_____
_____
_____
_____
_____
_____
_____
_____
_____
_____
_____
_____
_____

What are the names in your spouse's family that have a particular significance? Are there names that have been passed down through the generations?

_____

_____

_____

_____

_____

_____

_____

_____

_____

_____

_____

_____

_____

Are your children named for any family members on that side of the family? What is the significance of those names?

_____

_____

_____

_____

_____

_____

_____

_____

_____

_____

Do you remember if your grandparents had pets, or if your mom or dad had a favorite dog, cat, maybe even a horse growing up? What were those pets' names? Sometimes they are variations or nicknames associated with the family surname.

_____

_____

_____

_____

_____

_____

_____

_____

_____

_____

_____

Did you or do you have pets? Is there any special significance to the naming?

_____

_____

_____

_____

_____

_____

_____

_____

_____

_____

_____

CHAPTER THREE

Role Models: Getting to Know You

"People will not look forward to posterity, who never look backward to their ancestors."

—Edmund Burke

Role Models: Getting to Know You

Some of the most interesting insights into you come from uncovering and connecting the characteristics—appearance, personality, and style—that defined family members before you. These traits often can be connected to the traits you also share, or the intangible coincidences that match your current life. What were some of their natural talents, goals, dreams, and challenges your ancestors faced? The answers may reveal more about you and your vision.

_____

_____

_____

_____

_____

_____

Do you remember your grandparents or great-grandparents? What do you know about them?

_____

_____

_____

_____

_____

_____

_____

Who was the oldest person you can remember in your family as a child?
What do you remember about them?

_____

_____

_____

_____

_____

_____

What do you know about your great-grandparents on your mother's side? Where did they live as children, and what were their family lives like? How did their parents support their families?

_____

_____

_____

_____

_____

_____

_____

_____

_____

_____

What do you know about your great-grandparents on your dad's side? Again, where did that family live, and what was their lifestyle like? How did their parents support their families?

_____

_____

_____

_____

_____

_____

_____

_____

_____

_____

What personality traits, characteristics, or beliefs do family members say your great-grandparents on your mom's side have handed down through the generations?

_____

_____

_____

_____

_____

_____

_____

_____

_____

_____

What traits, characteristics, or beliefs are the legacy of your great-grandparents on your dad's side?

_____

_____

_____

_____

_____

_____

_____

_____

_____

_____

_____

"Our most basic instinct is not for survival but for family. Most of us would give our own life for the survival of a family member, yet we lead our daily life too often as if we take our family for granted."

—Paul Pearshall

Name one of the traits you admired about your grandmother on your mom's side. Name a trait that impressed you about your grandfather on your mom's side.

_____

_____

_____

_____

_____

_____

_____

_____

_____

_____

What was one of the traits you admired about your grandmother on your dad's side? What was one that impressed you about your grandfather on your dad's side?

_____

_____

_____

_____

_____

_____

_____

_____

_____

_____

_____

_____

Real Lives

Do you remember stories you heard about your grandparents? What do you know about them? What is your earliest memory of your grandparents? On your mom's side? On your dad's side?

_____

_____

_____

_____

_____

_____

_____

_____

_____

Do you remember hearing your grandparents describe their lives, or their parents' lives? What did they say?

_____

_____

_____

_____

_____

_____

_____

_____

_____

_____

What do you remember about your grandparents and their siblings, your great-aunts and great-uncles? Did you have a favorite one? Why?

_____

_____

_____

_____

_____

_____

_____

_____

_____

_____

_____

_____

Who represents the most positive role model for aging among your relatives? Why?

_____

_____

_____

_____

_____

_____

_____

_____

_____

_____

What "don't tell your mom this" secrets have your grandparents or aunts and uncles shared with you?

_____

_____

_____

_____

_____

_____

_____

_____

_____

_____

_____

Do you remember your family discussing world events and politics that influenced your grandparents' or great-grandparents' lives? What would you consider to be the most important inventions that have been made during their lifetimes?

_____

_____

_____

_____

_____

_____

_____

_____

_____

_____

_____

Life Lessons

Were you greatly influenced by one of your ancestors? What is the most important lesson one of your grandparents/parents taught you? Why? How did they exemplify it in their own lives?

_____

_____

_____

_____

_____

_____

_____

_____

_____

What struggles do you know your relatives went through? How did that inspire, encourage, or help you in your life?

_____

_____

_____

_____

_____

_____

_____

_____

_____

_____

"In a time of test, family is best."

—*Burmese proverb*

Who raised your mother, and what do you know about how she was raised? Was she raised in a home where there was a lot of economic stress or wealth? Was she expected to work to help make ends meet?

_____

_____

_____

_____

_____

_____

_____

_____

_____

_____

_____

Who raised your father? How was he brought up, and what was his childhood living environment like?

_____

_____

_____

_____

_____

_____

_____

_____

_____

_____

What a World

How do your parents and/or grandparents say the world now is different from what it was like when they were children?

_____

_____

_____

_____

_____

_____

_____

_____

_____

_____

Did your grandparents and parents share their philosophy of life with you, and what was it?

_____

_____

_____

_____

_____

_____

_____

_____

_____

_____

_____

*"There is nothing so annoying
as a good example!"*

—Mark Twain

Of all the things you learned from your parents/grandparents, which do you feel was the most valuable?

_____

_____

_____

_____

_____

_____

_____

_____

_____

_____

What lessons did they feel most strongly about passing along? What lessons are you passing on to your children?

_____

_____

_____

_____

_____

_____

_____

_____

_____

_____

_____

Share a special memory of your grandparents or of an older person you loved.

_____

_____

_____

_____

_____

_____

_____

_____

_____

_____

Is there an aunt, uncle, or close family friend who also inspires a special childhood memory?

_____

_____

_____

_____

_____

_____

_____

_____

_____

_____

_____

_____

"Blood's thicker than water, and when one's in trouble, best to seek out a relative's open arms."

—*Euripides*

Role Models

Which of their accomplishments would your grandparents/great-grandparents and parents say they were most proud?

_____

_____

_____

_____

_____

_____

_____

_____

_____

_____

_____

What role have those accomplishments played in inspiring your life goals?

_____

_____

_____

_____

_____

_____

_____

_____

_____

_____

_____

What were your parents' and grandparents' hobbies? Do you share any of these hobbies?

_____

_____

_____

_____

_____

_____

_____

_____

_____

_____

Are many members of your family in a particular profession or following a particular pursuit?

_____

_____

_____

_____

_____

_____

_____

_____

_____

_____

_____

_____

Did your parents or grandparents excel at a certain sport?

_____

_____

_____

_____

_____

Are there many people in your family who are ardent golfers?

_____

_____

_____

_____

_____

How about swimmers? Skiiers?

_____

_____

_____

_____

_____

Does anyone play football? Softball?

_____

_____

_____

_____

Do you or anyone in your family or extended family play a musical instrument? Do they entertain at family gatherings?

_____

_____

_____

_____

_____

_____

_____

_____

_____

Is there any special ability that seems to run in your family, such as a passion for reading or a talent for art? Has anyone in the family ever been recognized for these talents? If so, how?

_____

_____

_____

_____

_____

_____

_____

_____

_____

_____

_____

_____

Who is the best cook in the family? Are there any professional chefs?

_____

_____

_____

_____

_____

_____

_____

_____

_____

_____

Is there a craftsperson in the family? Is there any one who can knit, sew, or build things?

_____

_____

_____

_____

_____

_____

_____

_____

_____

_____

_____

Are there any of these distinguishing characteristics about your family that you share? Do people ever say you share the gift of gab, a sense of humor, or any other distinctive personality traits with your relatives or ancestors?

_____

_____

_____

_____

_____

_____

_____

_____

_____

_____

_____

_____

_____

Did anyone in the family have any particularly unusual characteristics?

_____

_____

_____

_____

_____

_____

_____

_____

_____

_____

_____

_____

How great are the physical resemblances in your family? Is there a certain feature, such as a facial feature, height, shape of head, etc., that many family members share?

_____

_____

_____

_____

_____

_____

_____

_____

Do you strongly resemble any particular members of your family?

_____

_____

_____

_____

_____

_____

_____

_____

_____

_____

_____

Is there a certain facial expression or gesture that many family members have?

_____

_____

_____

_____

_____

_____

_____

_____

_____

_____

Is there a verbal expression that many family members use?

_____

_____

_____

_____

_____

_____

_____

_____

_____

_____

_____

Secrets of Happiness

Do you have a particular passion that you share with your parents or family members? What is it, and how did they help inspire and mentor you in this?

_____

_____

_____

_____

_____

_____

_____

_____

_____

_____

What events and experiences with your family do you recall as having a major impact on your life?

_____

_____

_____

_____

_____

_____

_____

_____

_____

_____

_____

_____

Are there certain illnesses or health issues associated with your family?

_____

_____

_____

_____

_____

_____

_____

_____

_____

_____

Do you or your siblings have any of the health problems that affected your parents or grandparents?

_____

_____

_____

_____

_____

_____

_____

_____

_____

_____

_____

_____

"However time or circumstance may come between a mother and her child, their lives are interwoven forever."

—Pam Brown

Can you describe your father or mother as you remember seeing them when you were small?

_____

_____

_____

_____

_____

_____

_____

_____

_____

How did your mother spend her day? Did she stay at home, or did she work outside of the home?

_____

_____

_____

_____

_____

_____

_____

_____

_____

_____

_____

_____

Where did your father and/or mother go to work every day and what did they do?

_____

_____

_____

_____

_____

_____

_____

_____

_____

Did your father and/or mother have several different jobs? Did you ever move because of a parent's job?

_____

_____

_____

_____

_____

_____

_____

_____

_____

_____

_____

What wars have been fought during your family members' lifetimes? Did any of them serve in the military?

_____

_____

_____

_____

_____

_____

_____

_____

_____

_____

_____

If so, when and where did they serve, and what were their duties?

_____

_____

_____

_____

_____

_____

_____

_____

_____

_____

Did a family member become a war hero?

_____

_____

_____

_____

_____

_____

_____

_____

Did a family member die in combat? If so, when?

_____

_____

_____

_____

_____

_____

_____

_____

Was a family member seriously injured in wartime?

_____

_____

_____

_____

_____

_____

_____

If any of your grandparents have died, how old were you when they died?

_____

_____

_____

_____

_____

_____

_____

_____

_____

_____

Did they ever talk about their parents—where they came from, where they're buried?

_____

_____

_____

_____

_____

_____

_____

_____

_____

_____

Did your grandparents or great-grandparents speak a language other than English? Did they reminisce about life in "the old country"?

_____

_____

_____

_____

_____

_____

_____

_____

_____

_____

_____

What did they say it was like? Did they ever go back?

_____

_____

_____

_____

_____

_____

_____

_____

_____

_____

On the Sidelines

When you lost a sports game, weren't elected for class officer, or your friends ditched you as a child, how did your parents comfort you? What piece of advice did they have to offer you?

_____

_____

_____

_____

_____

_____

_____

_____

_____

_____

_____

_____

Did your parents then tell you about disappointments they had in their own childhoods? What were they? What lessons did they learn? What did that teach you?

_____

_____

_____

_____

_____

_____

_____

_____

_____

_____

"It is in the shelter of each other that people live."

—Irish proverb

What fads—popular hairstyles, clothes, etc.—have you heard were popular in your grandparents' day? What about your parents'?

_____

_____

_____

_____

_____

_____

_____

_____

_____

_____

_____

What music, clothing, hairstyles, etc., were popular when you were young? Do your children copy any of them today?

_____

_____

_____

_____

_____

_____

_____

_____

_____

_____

_____

Did your grandparents speak to you about the changes they have seen in the world?

_____

_____

_____

_____

_____

_____

_____

_____

_____

_____

_____

What changes did they especially like and dislike?

_____

_____

_____

_____

_____

_____

_____

_____

_____

_____

_____

Any adventurers in the family—family members who have fled the status quo to follow the bumper sticker calls: "I'd rather be sailing, . . . mountain climbing"?

_____

_____

_____

_____

_____

_____

_____

_____

_____

_____

_____

Did any of your relatives choose passion over security to pursue their purpose in life? If so, what did they do? How has that decision impacted or influenced your life?

_____

_____

_____

_____

_____

_____

_____

_____

_____

_____

Guess Who's Coming to Dinner

Can you remember an especially interesting family friend who visited or who was a frequent visitor to your home? What made that person or that occasion memorable?

_____

_____

_____

_____

_____

_____

_____

_____

_____

_____

What was the silliest thing you ever saw one of your older relatives do? Why was it so funny?

_____

_____

_____

_____

_____

_____

_____

_____

_____

_____

_____

Were there any well-known people or celebrities in your family?

_____

_____

_____

_____

_____

_____

_____

_____

_____

_____

_____

What made them famous?

_____

_____

_____

_____

_____

_____

_____

_____

_____

_____

_____

With or without the recognition, did any people in your family exhibit extraordinary abilities?

_____

_____

_____

_____

_____

_____

_____

_____

_____

_____

_____

What admirable qualities do you find in some of the people in your family? Were you ever touched by an act of kindness shown by this person?

_____

_____

_____

_____

_____

_____

_____

_____

_____

_____

_____

From the Heart

Did your relatives practice a particular religion? Do you practice it today? Why or why not?

_____

_____

_____

_____

_____

_____

_____

_____

_____

_____

What about your spouse's family? What is their religious heritage?

_____

_____

_____

_____

_____

_____

_____

_____

_____

_____

Many families in America are mixed marriages, where people of different religious, ethnic, or racial backgrounds decide to wed. Do you have these in your family?

_____

_____

_____

_____

_____

_____

_____

_____

_____

_____

_____

Has your family accepted or rejected this marriage and relationship?

_____

_____

_____

_____

_____

_____

_____

_____

_____

_____

_____

_____

Were there clerics, people of God, or missionaries in your family? Where did they serve?

_____

_____

_____

_____

_____

_____

_____

_____

_____

_____

_____

Did your family produce any scholars or scientists?

_____

_____

_____

_____

_____

_____

_____

_____

_____

What level of education did your parents and grandparents have? Did any have advanced degrees?

_____

_____

_____

_____

_____

_____

_____

_____

_____

_____

Have they passed that thirst for knowledge down to you and your children?

_____

_____

_____

_____

_____

_____

_____

_____

_____

_____

_____

"Example is a bright looking-glass,
universal and for all shapes to look into."

—Michel De Montaigne

Memories

List one special memory about each of your brothers and sisters.

_____

_____

_____

_____

_____

_____

_____

_____

_____

_____

_____

_____

_____

_____

_____

_____

_____

_____

_____

_____

_____

_____

New Spouse/Stepfamilies, etc.

What are the qualities belonging to your stepmom or stepdad, second wife or husband, that make up their inherent character?

_____

_____

_____

_____

_____

_____

_____

_____

_____

_____

Where were they born?

_____

_____

_____

_____

_____

_____

_____

_____

_____

What are their unique personality traits?

_____
_____
_____
_____
_____
_____
_____
_____
_____
_____
_____
_____

What are their sisters and brothers like?

_____
_____
_____
_____
_____
_____
_____
_____
_____
_____
_____
_____

How did you meet your new spouse/stepdad or stepmom?

_____

_____

_____

_____

_____

_____

_____

_____

_____

_____

_____

_____

Does he or she have children? What are their names and ages? Where were they born?

_____

_____

_____

_____

_____

_____

_____

_____

_____

_____

How have you blended this stepfamily into your existing one? Do you live with your stepsiblings in the same house?

_____

_____

_____

_____

_____

_____

_____

_____

_____

_____

What traits do your stepsiblings share with you? Or, what makes them completely different from you? What are their names? How do they differ in age from you?

_____

_____

_____

_____

_____

_____

_____

_____

_____

_____

_____

Do your mom and stepdad, or dad and stepmom, have any children—your stepsisters or stepbrothers—by their new marriage? How do they tell you that child or those children are like you?

_____

_____

_____

_____

_____

_____

_____

_____

_____

What trait do you admire most about your stepmom or stepfather? What new traditions is he/she bringing into your family, and how do they play out?

_____

_____

_____

_____

_____

_____

_____

_____

_____

_____

Who are your stepgrandparents, and what are they like?

_____

_____

_____

_____

_____

_____

_____

How many other grandchildren do they have?

_____

_____

_____

_____

_____

_____

_____

_____

Where were they born? What nationality are they?

_____

_____

_____

_____

_____

_____

Cousins

Did your cousins play an important role in your life? How?

_____

_____

_____

_____

_____

_____

_____

_____

_____

_____

_____

Who in this category has influenced your life profoundly? In what way?

_____

_____

_____

_____

_____

_____

_____

_____

_____

_____

List three words or phrases that describe the personalities of each your family members, starting with your grandparents and including your parents, aunts and uncles, yourself, your siblings, and your children. What are the similarities? Differences?

_____

_____

_____

_____

_____

_____

_____

_____

_____

_____

_____

Do you notice any connections between the generations?

_____

_____

_____

_____

_____

_____

_____

_____

_____

_____

_____

_____

Secrets

Are there any family secrets?

_____
_____
_____
_____
_____
_____
_____
_____
_____
_____
_____
_____
_____
_____
_____
_____
_____
_____
_____
_____
_____
_____
_____
_____
_____
_____
_____

Every family has black sheep. Who are the black sheep in your family? Do you talk about them?

_____
_____
_____
_____
_____
_____
_____
_____
_____
_____
_____

Did a close relative have trouble with the law?

_____
_____
_____
_____
_____
_____
_____
_____
_____
_____
_____

What characteristics—physical, emotional, spiritual or intellectual—have your children inherited from you or from other family members?

_____

_____

_____

_____

_____

_____

_____

_____

_____

_____

_____

_____

_____

_____

_____

_____

_____

_____

_____

_____

_____

_____

_____

_____

_____

CHAPTER FOUR

Location, Location: Ties That Bind

"We shape our dwellings, and afterwards, our dwellings shape us."

— Winston Churchill

Location, Location: Ties that Bind

To know your ancestors, it is important to create a visual picture of where they lived and what their ancestral home looked and felt like. It may be relatively easy to describe your ancestors' environment, but if you've never been there, or heard about it, it's also not too hard to research. You can contact the local office of tourism for brochures and see if there is a virtual tour online. Also, now is the time to pull out the family photo albums, scrapbooks, and other telling mementos. At the same time, it's important to look at your own family home and what it reveals about you.

_____

_____

_____

_____

_____

_____

_____

_____

_____

_____

_____

_____

_____

_____

_____

_____

_____

_____

_____

_____

This Old House

Describe the houses in which your grandparents and, if you know, great-grandparents lived when they were children. Any similarities between the generations?

_____

_____

_____

_____

_____

_____

_____

_____

_____

_____

Were they born in other parts of the world? Where? What were their childhood homes and neighborhoods like?

_____

_____

_____

_____

_____

_____

_____

_____

_____

_____

_____

"Home is a name, a word, it is a strong one; stronger than magician ever spoke, or spirit ever answered to, in the strongest conjuration."

—Charles Dickens

Where were your grandparents, great-grandparents, and parents born?

_____

_____

_____

_____

_____

_____

_____

_____

_____

_____

_____

Share some stories they told you about being a child and growing up in the part of the world, city, or neighborhood where they lived.

_____

_____

_____

_____

_____

_____

_____

_____

_____

_____

_____

_____

_____

Do you remember your grandparents' homes? What special memories do you have there?

_____

_____

_____

_____

_____

_____

_____

_____

_____

_____

_____

Where were your parents born? How do they describe the homes they grew up in and what their neighborhoods were like?

_____

_____

_____

_____

_____

_____

_____

_____

_____

_____

Have you ever gone to visit the country, city, or hometown where your grandparents or great-grandparents lived as children? How did it feel to you?

_____

_____

_____

_____

_____

_____

_____

_____

_____

_____

_____

What about your parents' childhood homes? Have you ever been there to visit?

_____

_____

_____

_____

_____

_____

_____

_____

_____

_____

_____

"A comfortable house is a great source of happiness. It ranks immediately after health and a good conscience."

— Sydney Smith

In what place were you born? When?

_____

_____

_____

_____

_____

_____

_____

_____

_____

_____

_____

Where was your childhood home located? Did you enjoy living there?

_____

_____

_____

_____

_____

_____

_____

_____

_____

_____

_____

_____

Was your first childhood home a house, an apartment, a farm? How many rooms were there?

_____

_____

_____

_____

_____

_____

_____

_____

_____

Were there any special items or features in the home that you remember?

_____

_____

_____

_____

_____

_____

_____

_____

_____

Trading Spaces

How many homes did you live in when you were growing up? Did your family move often?

_____

_____

_____

_____

_____

_____

_____

_____

_____

_____

_____

If your family did move often, where did you live, and in what time periods?

_____

_____

_____

_____

_____

_____

_____

_____

_____

_____

Is there a home that was or has been in your family for a long time?

_____

_____

_____

_____

_____

_____

_____

_____

_____

_____

_____

Who lives there now?

_____

_____

_____

_____

_____

_____

_____

_____

_____

_____

Was there one home that you especially liked? Especially disliked?

_____

_____

_____

_____

_____

_____

_____

_____

_____

_____

_____

Who lived in your home with you as a child? How many brothers or sisters lived there?
Did any grandparents, aunts and uncles, or other relatives live with you?

_____

_____

_____

_____

_____

_____

_____

_____

_____

_____

Who frequently visited your home when you were young? Was it a place where friends and relatives gathered?

_____

_____

_____

_____

_____

_____

_____

_____

_____

_____

_____

Describe your favorite memories of gatherings at your childhood home. Who was there?

_____

_____

_____

_____

_____

_____

_____

_____

_____

_____

_____

Describe your childhood bedroom. What was the view from your window?

_____

_____

_____

_____

_____

_____

_____

_____

_____

_____

Did you have your own bedroom, or did you share one? What special memories do you have in that room?

_____

_____

_____

_____

_____

_____

_____

_____

_____

_____

"Close your eyes, tap your heels together three times, and think to yourself, There's no place like home."

— <u>The Wizard of Oz</u>, movie directed by Victor Fleming, based on a novel by L. Frank Baum

In your childhood home, did you have a family room? What did it look like?

_____

_____

_____

_____

_____

_____

_____

_____

_____

_____

Did your home contain a playroom?

_____

_____

_____

_____

_____

_____

_____

_____

_____

_____

_____

Did your family gather in the living room? Or, was the dining room or the kitchen the focal point?

_____

_____

_____

_____

_____

_____

_____

_____

_____

_____

_____

Was any room "off-limits"—to be avoided by children who might mess it up?

_____

_____

_____

_____

_____

_____

_____

_____

_____

_____

Is there a particular room that has special significance? A library? Does your family love to read?

_____

_____

_____

_____

_____

_____

_____

_____

_____

Did your home have a beautiful lawn? A spectacular garden? Did you (do you) share a green thumb with anyone in your family?

_____

_____

_____

_____

_____

_____

_____

_____

_____

_____

_____

_____

Did your childhood home have a yard?

_____

_____

_____

_____

_____

_____

_____

Did you have trees to climb?

_____

_____

_____

_____

_____

_____

_____

_____

Was there a park or any open space nearby?

_____

_____

_____

_____

_____

_____

_____

Hideaways

Did you ever have a special hideaway or playhouse? What made it special?

_____

_____

_____

_____

_____

_____

_____

_____

_____

_____

_____

What is your fondest memory of your childhood home? Your grandparents' home?

_____

_____

_____

_____

_____

_____

_____

_____

_____

_____

How did your family come to live in your childhood home? Did any other family members live nearby? Cousins, aunts, uncles, grandparents?

_____
_____
_____
_____
_____
_____
_____
_____
_____
_____
_____

Who were your favorite neighbors?

_____
_____
_____
_____
_____
_____
_____
_____
_____
_____
_____

What special memory do you have about a neighborhood experience? Did you hold block parties or other gatherings? How many kids grew up on the block where you lived?

_____

_____

_____

_____

_____

_____

_____

_____

Were there any other special neighborhood events?

_____

_____

_____

_____

_____

_____

_____

Where did you go for fun and recreation? Neighborhood park? Pool? A vacant lot? Etc.?

_____

_____

_____

_____

_____

_____

_____

School Days

How far did you have to travel to attend school and how did you get there?

_____

_____

_____

_____

_____

_____

_____

_____

Did you attend the same school as other members of your family?

_____

_____

_____

_____

_____

_____

_____

_____

Did your parents or older relatives attend the same school?

_____

_____

_____

_____

_____

_____

_____

*"In search of my mother's garden,
I found my own."*

—Alice Walker

What kind of car did your family drive? Were you proud of it or embarrassed by it? Why?

_____

_____

_____

_____

_____

_____

_____

Did your family change cars often? Did you always have a new car, or did you ride around in old beat-up cars, hoping they would last until your family found a better one?

_____

_____

_____

_____

_____

_____

Is any family member good at fixing cars? Did any become mechanics?

_____

_____

_____

_____

_____

_____

_____

What is your home like today? Does it include any furniture or heirlooms from your ancestors?

_____

_____

_____

_____

_____

_____

_____

_____

_____

_____

Are there things in your home you may be able to pass on to your children, siblings, or friends that will carry a special significance for them forever?

_____

_____

_____

_____

_____

_____

_____

_____

_____

_____

_____

"The informality of family life is a blessed condition that allows us to become our best while looking our worst."

—*Marge Kennedy*

Where do your siblings live? How do their homes or neighborhoods reflect your childhood experiences?

_____

_____

_____

_____

_____

_____

_____

_____

_____

Do you live near any childhood friends or friends of your family? Do the generations continue to get together?

_____

_____

_____

_____

_____

_____

_____

_____

_____

_____

_____

Family Vacations

Where did you go on family vacations? Who went with you? What did you do for fun?

_____

_____

_____

_____

_____

_____

_____

_____

_____

_____

_____

Did you visit other relatives? Where did they live?

_____

_____

_____

_____

_____

_____

_____

_____

_____

_____

_____

Did you family have a summer home? A usual vacation spot?

_____

_____

_____

_____

_____

_____

_____

_____

_____

_____

_____

Did your family go on camping trips?

_____

_____

_____

_____

_____

_____

_____

_____

_____

_____

_____

_____

What was your favorite family vacation? Where did you go and why was it special?

_____

_____

_____

_____

_____

_____

_____

_____

_____

What is the longest trip that you have ever been on? Where did you go?

_____

_____

_____

_____

_____

_____

_____

_____

_____

"In each family a story is playing itself out, and each family's story embodies its hope and despair."

— *Auguste Napier*

Reality TV

Did you have a television in your family home? What were your family's favorite programs?

_____

_____

_____

_____

_____

_____

_____

_____

_____

_____

_____

Were there shows that your family regularly watched together?

_____

_____

_____

_____

_____

_____

_____

_____

_____

_____

Did you have any games or hobbies you shared with your family members as a child?

_____

_____

_____

_____

_____

_____

_____

_____

_____

_____

_____

Did you and your siblings have to do childhood chores, and how did you split them up?

_____

_____

_____

_____

_____

_____

_____

_____

_____

_____

_____

Did your family have many pets?

_____
_____
_____
_____
_____
_____
_____
_____
_____
_____

What was your favorite family pet? Why was it your favorite?

_____
_____
_____
_____
_____
_____
_____
_____
_____
_____
_____

CHAPTER FIVE

You've Got to Have Friends and Mentors

"Each friend is indeed a world—a special sphere of certain emotions, experiences, memories and qualities of personality. We are all made up of many worlds and each friendship brings one or more of these worlds to life."

— *Thomas Moore*

You've Got to Have Friends and Mentors

Which neighbors did you borrow a cup of sugar from? Who kept a spare key, watered the garden, and watched the house while you vacationed? Who took care of the children and who brought supper in times of need? Sometimes family become friends, and many times there are friends who share our lives and legacies, becoming extended family. Sometimes we are lucky to have pivotal others—teachers, a church leader, neighbor, scout leader, or coach—who help us reach our hopes and dreams. In this chapter we ask you to look at and reflect upon the significant others who have played key roles in your family's life.

Who were your parents' friends? What did you like most about them?

_____

_____

_____

_____

_____

_____

_____

_____

_____

_____

What made these people so special? Why, out of all the people your family knew, did you form a special attachment to these people?

_____

_____

_____

_____

_____

_____

_____

_____

_____

_____

_____

Divine Rights

Is there any person who has become an honorary family member of yours over the years? Who? How did you meet, and how did this person become an integral part of your family?

_____

_____

_____

_____

_____

_____

_____

_____

_____

_____

Were you ever selected as a godparent or honorary aunt or uncle for a friend's child? How did this make you feel? What kind of adult has this child become today?

_____

_____

_____

_____

_____

_____

_____

_____

_____

_____

_____

The Pleasure of Their Company

Describe a memorable holiday or event where your family's friends joined in the celebration.

_____

_____

_____

_____

_____

_____

_____

_____

_____

Did that person introduce a new tradition, recipe, or way of doing things to that occasion and how did they make it special?

_____

_____

_____

_____

_____

_____

_____

_____

_____

_____

_____

_____

Make a list of the people you are most grateful for—your neighbors, relatives, those who have made your life meaningful, joyous, and fun.

_____

_____

_____

_____

_____

_____

_____

_____

_____

_____

_____

How did these people impact your life?

_____

_____

_____

_____

_____

_____

_____

_____

_____

_____

_____

_____

_____

Wonder Women, Super Men

Who were the people who had the most influence on your early adulthood? An older sibling, a coach, a professor, a friend of the family?

_____

_____

_____

_____

_____

_____

_____

_____

_____

_____

Who were the people who shaped you in the following areas: Major at college? Career? Relationships? Faith? Describe these people and how they helped you find meaning in your young adult life.

_____

_____

_____

_____

_____

_____

_____

_____

_____

_____

_____

Haul out the old family photo albums and look at the pictures of your mom and dad, of your grandma and grandpa as children and experiencing the special life events. Who are the friends who were nearest and dearest to them?

_____

_____

_____

_____

_____

_____

_____

_____

_____

_____

What did they tell you about those people? Are any of them people you call "aunts" or "uncles" because they played such a significant role in an ancestor's life?

_____

_____

_____

_____

_____

_____

_____

_____

_____

_____

_____

_____

"Friendship is the only thing in the world concerning the usefulness of which all mankind are agreed."

—Cicero

Do you have a family Bible in which events are recorded? Who is the keeper of the family facts?

_____

_____

_____

_____

_____

_____

_____

_____

_____

Do you have a person in your family whom others consider the "family historian"?

_____

_____

_____

_____

_____

_____

_____

_____

_____

_____

Pull out your baby book or scrapbook. Who are the people in the photographs—aunts, uncles, grandparents, godparents, cousins?

_____

_____

_____

_____

_____

_____

_____

_____

_____

What memories do you have of those family gatherings, vacations, or events? Who was there, and what do you remember about those people?

_____

_____

_____

_____

_____

_____

_____

_____

_____

_____

_____

_____

Do you have a favorite aunt, uncle, or cousin? What is it about that person that makes them special?

_____

_____

_____

_____

_____

_____

_____

_____

_____

Did they share a particular pastime with you? What was it, and what are some of your happiest memories from those times?

_____

_____

_____

_____

_____

_____

_____

_____

_____

_____

_____

Circle of Friends

The baseball buddies. The neighbors who played cards at your house. Carpool and commuting companions. Church social groups. Who were the everyday friends of your mom and dad, and what do you remember that was so special about them?

_____

_____

_____

_____

_____

_____

_____

_____

_____

_____

_____

Do you have similar friends in your life today?

_____

_____

_____

_____

_____

_____

_____

_____

_____

_____

_____

Did your parents or grandparents ever open their homes to strangers, people who were alone for the holidays and needed a friend?

_____
_____
_____
_____
_____
_____
_____
_____
_____
_____

How did those people brighten your celebrations?

_____
_____
_____
_____
_____
_____
_____
_____
_____
_____
_____
_____

As a young person did you participate in any religious groups, scout troops, or teams where the leaders played a strong role in influencing your life?

_____

_____

_____

_____

_____

_____

_____

_____

_____

_____

_____

_____

Who were these people? Share a little about how they inspired you.

_____

_____

_____

_____

_____

_____

_____

_____

_____

_____

_____

_____

"Old friends are the blessings
of a long life."

— *Scottish proverb*

Best Friends

Who was your best childhood friend? Do you remember the day you first met?

_____

_____

_____

_____

_____

_____

_____

_____

_____

_____

What did you enjoy doing with this person the most?

_____

_____

_____

_____

_____

_____

_____

_____

_____

_____

_____

"The real mirror of your life and soul is your true friend. A friend helps you glimpse who you really are and what you are doing here."

—John O'Donohue

CHAPTER SIX

Transitions: Navigating Life Events

"Family life is full of major and minor crises—the ups and downs of health, success and failure in career, marriage, and divorce—and all kinds of characters. It is tied to places and events and histories. With all of these felt details, life etches itself into memory and personality. It's difficult to imagine anything more nourishing to the soul."

—Thomas Moore

Transitions: Navigating Life Events

The only constant in life is change. Change from childhood to adulthood, from being single to being married, from work to retirement, from the family home to a retirement home. The passage from one phase of life to another always includes a period of transition. We look forward to exciting new opportunities, but are apprehensive about leaving what we know. That is why the stories we need to hear about our families—and our children need to hear from us—are not the stories of daunting success, impressive achievements, or dazzling accomplishment. Wisdom comes from understanding and revealing the periods of transition. If we look back at how our relatives faced the challenges and changes in their lives, it gives us inspiration to look forward to our own futures, and our children's.

_____

_____

_____

_____

_____

_____

_____

_____

_____

_____

_____

_____

_____

_____

_____

_____

_____

_____

_____

_____

_____

_____

Close Encounters

Do you know how your grandparents met each other? Your great-grandparents?

_____

_____

_____

_____

_____

_____

_____

How did your parents meet each other? How old were they when they started dating?

_____

_____

_____

_____

_____

_____

_____

_____

How did you meet your spouse or significant other? Any similarities?

_____

_____

_____

_____

_____

_____

_____

_____

How did your grandfather(s) propose to your grandmother(s)? How did your dad ask your mom to marry him? How were you proposed to?

_____

_____

_____

_____

_____

_____

_____

_____

Describe your grandparents' and parents' weddings. Who was there? Where were they held? Were any traditions started at their weddings that are carried on in your family today?

_____

_____

_____

_____

_____

_____

_____

_____

_____

"Call it a clan, call it a network, call it a tribe, and call it a family: Whatever you call it, whoever you are, you need one."

— Jane Howard

Making Fun

What did your mom and her siblings do when they were bored? What do you know about their childhood toys?

_____
_____
_____
_____
_____
_____
_____
_____
_____
_____
_____

What do you know about their crushes? Their adult embarrassments? Relationships?

_____
_____
_____
_____
_____
_____
_____
_____
_____
_____
_____

What about your dad and his brothers and sisters? What do you know about their childhood toys?

_____

_____

_____

_____

_____

_____

_____

_____

_____

_____

What do you know about their crushes? Their adult embarrassments? Relationships?

_____

_____

_____

_____

_____

_____

_____

_____

_____

_____

_____

What would your mom and dad say their greatest achievements were?

_____

_____

_____

_____

_____

_____

_____

_____

_____

_____

_____

What time in their lives would your parents say was their hardest? Why? What was their greatest loss? How did they overcome this? And how did it impact you?

_____

_____

_____

_____

_____

_____

_____

_____

_____

_____

_____

_____

_____

"Everything in life that we really accept undergoes a change."

— Katherine Mansfield

Gifts from the Heart

How did your grandparents pass down their spiritual heritage to your parents and to you? What piece of wisdom that came from the heart did they share with you?

_____

_____

_____

_____

_____

_____

_____

_____

_____

_____

Do you remember a time when you were younger that something sad or disappointing happened to you, and your grandparents or parents shared their hard-earned wisdom to help you get through the difficult time?

_____

_____

_____

_____

_____

_____

_____

_____

_____

Did your family go through any major upheaval when you were a child, such as a divorce, job loss, and death in the family? How did this affect you at the time? What life lessons has it taught you?

_____

_____

_____

_____

_____

_____

_____

_____

_____

_____

Can you remember any particularly happy time in your family life? Describe how you felt about it then, and how it makes you feel today.

_____

_____

_____

_____

_____

_____

_____

_____

_____

_____

_____

Do you remember when your siblings were born? How did you feel?
How old were you when they were born? What family stories do you remember
surrounding their births?

_____

_____

_____

_____

_____

_____

_____

_____

_____

_____

Does your birth order, or that of your siblings, tell anything about your personalities?

_____

_____

_____

_____

_____

_____

_____

_____

_____

_____

_____

_____

Teacher, Teacher

Where did you go to grade school? What is your strongest school memory?

_____

_____

_____

_____

_____

_____

Who was your favorite teacher? What subject did that person teach, and how did he or she draw out your talents in the class?

_____

_____

_____

_____

_____

_____

_____

What school activities and sports did you participate in? Were you ever given any special awards for your studies or school activities?

_____

_____

_____

_____

_____

_____

Did you get good grades? Did you like school?

_____

_____

_____

_____

_____

_____

_____

Do you have a mentor, someone who has guided you through school or your career? Describe that person.

_____

_____

_____

_____

_____

_____

_____

How many years of education have you completed? Do you have a college degree? If so, what was your field of study?

_____

_____

_____

_____

_____

_____

_____

The Dating Game

How old were you when you started dating? Do you remember your first date?

_____

_____

_____

_____

_____

_____

_____

How did you meet your spouse and/or significant other?

_____

_____

_____

_____

_____

_____

_____

What was it like when your spouse proposed to you? When and where did it happen? How?

_____

_____

_____

_____

_____

_____

_____

_____

_____

Wedding Day

Where and when did you get married? What memory stands out from your wedding day?

_____

_____

_____

_____

_____

_____

_____

How would you describe your wedding ceremony? Celebration? Who stood up at your wedding? Where did you go on your honeymoon?

_____

_____

_____

_____

_____

_____

_____

Have you been married more than once?

_____

_____

_____

_____

_____

_____

_____

"We cannot destroy kindred:
our chains stretch a little sometimes,
but they never break."

— Marquise de Sevigne

Career
What is your profession and how did you choose it?

_____

_____

_____

_____

_____

_____

_____

_____

_____

_____

What accomplishments are you most proud of?

_____

_____

_____

_____

_____

_____

_____

_____

_____

Which relatives were at all your major life events? What do you remember about their presence? Were you at their special events?

_____

_____

_____

_____

_____

_____

_____

_____

_____

_____

Who is your closest cousin or aunt or uncle and why?

_____

_____

_____

_____

_____

_____

_____

_____

_____

_____

_____

_____

_____

People Who Make a Difference

How have your relationships to your closest relatives grown or evolved over the years? Which of your family relationships has changed the most significantly in your adult life? Is it the one you have with a parent, sibling, aunt, uncle, cousin? How would you describe that relationship, as it was years ago, and how it stands today?

_____

_____

_____

_____

_____

_____

_____

_____

_____

_____

_____

_____

_____

_____

_____

_____

_____

_____

_____

_____

_____

_____

CHAPTER SEVEN

Family Stories

"*In my family, questions about the living of life, especially those pertaining to matters of the heart and soul, are most often answered by telling stories or a series of tales.*"

—Clarissa Pinkola Estes

Family Stories

What stories have been passed down to you about your parents? Grandparents? Great-grandparents? Do your grandmother and grandfather, mother and father, aunts and uncles, tell stories about the "good old days"? Family stories shape and define who we are. In this chapter we invite you to pay closer attention to them.

Every family has its family legend: a story that has been passed down at bedtime from parent to child for generations. In these stories, ancestors sometimes have accomplished amazing feats—first man to climb Mt. Everest, a bohemian who ran away to Paris to paint world-famous artwork…. You get the picture. What is your family legend? Write it down here.

_____

_____

_____

_____

_____

_____

_____

_____

_____

_____

_____

_____

_____

_____

_____

_____

_____

_____

_____

_____

_____

In your family legend, who was the character you most identified with and what was your favorite part of the story? Was there a moral to the story? If so, what was it and why do you remember it?

_____

_____

_____

_____

_____

_____

_____

_____

_____

_____

_____

_____

How much of this story do you think is factual, and how much is fiction? If this story is based on actual facts, what were they?

_____

_____

_____

_____

_____

_____

_____

_____

_____

_____

_____

_____

Telling Tales

Do your aunts and uncles tell stories about your mom and dad? What are they?

_____

_____

_____

_____

_____

_____

_____

_____

_____

_____

Is there a family immigration story? Harrowing event of travel from "the old country" to America? Share this.

_____

_____

_____

_____

_____

_____

_____

_____

_____

_____

Do your elders talk about going to school? The fun they had with friends? Family celebrations and holidays? Picnics on the Fourth of July? What are their stories?

_____

_____

_____

_____

_____

_____

_____

_____

_____

_____

Is there a love story that is passed down through the generations of your family—how your grandparents met, or a funny blind date story?

_____

_____

_____

_____

_____

_____

_____

_____

_____

_____

_____

_____

"We are all omnibuses in which our ancestors ride, and every now and then one of them sticks his head out and embarrasses us."

— Oliver Wendell Holmes

Grandma Says . . .

Are there any particular sayings you remember your grandparents or relatives repeating often? What are the catchphrases, and when did they usually come up in conversations?

_____

_____

_____

_____

_____

_____

_____

_____

_____

_____

Why do you think these sayings were so relevant to your family back when? Which saying still holds true today?

_____

_____

_____

_____

_____

_____

_____

_____

_____

_____

_____

_____

_____

Do they ever tell tales of distant ancestors who were famous, or infamous? What are they?

_____
_____
_____
_____
_____
_____
_____
_____
_____
_____

It seems like every family has fascinating stories about an ancestor who has a very "interesting" or spotted past. Who was the wild ancestor who stirred up the family pot? What did this person do?

_____
_____
_____
_____
_____
_____
_____
_____
_____
_____

Mighty Myths

What are some of the other outlandish stories you have heard about ancestors? Is there a myth about an ancestor? An aunt who was an Indian princess, a great uncle who ran away to the circus?

_____

_____

_____

_____

_____

_____

_____

_____

_____

_____

Are there relatives who played a role in history? Actors? Writers? Athletes? Who are your most notable ancestors?

_____

_____

_____

_____

_____

_____

_____

_____

_____

_____

"They . . . threw themselves into the interests of the rest, but each plowed his or her own furrow. Their thoughts, their little passions and hopes and desires, all ran along separate lines. Family life is like this—animated, but collateral."

— Rose Macaulay

Voyages

What are the stories that have been shared about your immigrant ancestors and their pilgrimage to the United States?

_____

_____

_____

_____

_____

_____

_____

_____

_____

_____

_____

Do you know what happened to the ancestors who stayed behind in their native homeland?

_____

_____

_____

_____

_____

_____

_____

_____

_____

_____

_____

Do you have an entrepreneurial ancestor who amassed great fortune from an invention or new business idea? Who was it and what was it?

_____

_____

_____

_____

_____

_____

_____

_____

_____

What kind of reputation did your family have in your grandparents' day? How do you think they earned this reputation?

_____

_____

_____

_____

_____

_____

_____

_____

_____

_____

_____

Did any of your ancestors overcome extraordinary challenges?

_____

_____

_____

_____

_____

_____

_____

Did any of your ancestors endure extreme hardships?

_____

_____

_____

_____

_____

_____

_____

What have you learned about your ancestors and family that makes you proud?

_____

_____

_____

_____

_____

_____

_____

_____

"In our family an experience was not finished, nor truly experienced, unless written down or shared with another."

— Anne Morrow Lindbergh

Sibling Secrets

Do your aunts and uncles have any good stories to share about your parents' childhoods? How they behaved at school? The times they got in trouble with their parents?

_____

_____

_____

_____

_____

_____

_____

_____

_____

What secret stories about your own childhood do you have?

_____

_____

_____

_____

_____

_____

_____

_____

_____

_____

What stories do your parents share about the day of or the circumstances of your birth? Your siblings?

_____

_____

_____

_____

_____

_____

_____

_____

_____

_____

_____

What are their favorite memories of your childhood?

_____

_____

_____

_____

_____

_____

_____

_____

_____

_____

_____

What are the favorite books from your childhood that were read to you by your parents or grandparents?

_____

_____

_____

_____

_____

_____

_____

_____

_____

_____

What books or stories do you pass on to your children or nieces and nephews today?

_____

_____

_____

_____

_____

_____

_____

_____

_____

_____

_____

_____

"Family faces are magic mirrors. Looking at people who belong to us, we see the past, present, and future."

— Gail Lumet Buckley

CHAPTER EIGHT

Tradition, Tradition

"*Our lives make sense in a thousand ways, most of which we are unaware of, because of traditions that are centuries if not millennia old. It is these traditions that help us to know that it does make a difference who we are and how we treat one another.*"

— Robert Bellah

Ritual and tradition are important elements of human life. Traditions connect the participants in a common endeavor (such as being a family) with a common goal. As folklorist Steven J. Zeitlin says, "Traditions are glue, the common ground around which a family revolves." Traditions that continue customs started by your ancestors are priceless. They link you to your relatives in a real and palpable way, creating an appreciation of their lives and an awareness of their legacies to you and your children. It's reassuring to have traditions that a family can depend on always to remain the same. In this chapter, collect the enduring pleasures that came from everyday and special rituals and traditions in your family.

_____

_____

_____

_____

_____

_____

_____

_____

_____

_____

_____

_____

_____

_____

_____

_____

_____

_____

_____

_____

Everyday Rituals

What are some of the everyday rituals you remember from your childhood? Eating dinner together as a family? Bedtime rituals, such as telling stories, praying together, or listening to music?

_____

_____

_____

_____

_____

_____

_____

_____

_____

_____

What did those rituals mean and have you carried on any of them today?

_____

_____

_____

_____

_____

_____

_____

_____

_____

_____

Was there any religious ritual or practice your family observed on a daily basis? What about on a weekly basis, or on holidays?

_____

_____

_____

_____

_____

_____

_____

_____

How do you remember feeling about this practice at the time? Do you still do it today?

_____

_____

_____

_____

_____

_____

_____

_____

_____

_____

_____

What kind of prayer did you say before you went to sleep? Or did your parents sing a special lullaby or song to you?

_____

_____

_____

_____

_____

_____

_____

_____

_____

Who taught you to give thanks in your life?

_____

_____

_____

_____

_____

_____

_____

_____

_____

_____

_____

_____

Tell about a special outing you took with your mother or father.

_____

_____

_____

_____

_____

_____

_____

_____

_____

_____

_____

Do you have a special place you take your children, nieces, nephews, or family friends today?

_____

_____

_____

_____

_____

_____

_____

_____

_____

_____

_____

_____

_____

What did your family do on weekends? Was there a favorite outing? A ride in the car in the country? A trek to Grandma's? Going into the city to a museum?

_____

_____

_____

_____

_____

_____

_____

_____

_____

_____

What did you do in the summertime? What summer stands out as the most memorable in your childhood? Describe.

_____

_____

_____

_____

_____

_____

_____

_____

_____

_____

_____

_____

Makes Scents

What scent or sound takes you immediately back to your childhood? What feelings and memories does it evoke?

_____

_____

_____

_____

_____

_____

_____

_____

_____

Is there a particular style of decorating with flowers or using other special touches which your parents or grandparents created that made every occasion more special?

_____

_____

_____

_____

_____

_____

_____

_____

_____

_____

_____

_____

Did you do any volunteering as a family in your community?

_____

_____

_____

_____

_____

_____

_____

_____

_____

_____

_____

Do you remember how you felt helping those people? Has it inspired you to volunteer today?

_____

_____

_____

_____

_____

_____

_____

_____

_____

_____

_____

_____

The Write Stuff

We have endured several wars in the last centuries. Did you have ancestors who served in the military? Did any of them face combat or die in wartime?

_____

_____

_____

_____

_____

_____

_____

_____

_____

What was their memory of living through that period in history? Did they communicate their feelings about the war in letters to others?

_____

_____

_____

_____

_____

_____

_____

_____

_____

_____

What were some of your family rituals for keeping in touch, such as sending family letters and holding family reunions?

_____

_____

_____

_____

_____

_____

_____

_____

_____

_____

What new traditions would you like to start in your own family based on your childhood?

_____

_____

_____

_____

_____

_____

_____

_____

_____

_____

_____

_____

_____

It's Your Party

Did you have any birthday rituals, such as serving breakfast in bed to the birthday person or making his or her favorite meal? How did you celebrate birthdays? Who made the cake?

_____

_____

_____

_____

_____

_____

_____

_____

_____

What was one of your favorite birthday parties? Who was there, and what did you do?

_____

_____

_____

_____

_____

_____

_____

_____

_____

_____

"Tradition is a guide and not a jailer."

—William Somerset Maugham

Holiday Traditions and Rituals

Describe some of your holiday traditions, such as creating handmade ornaments for Christmas, lighting the menorah together, organizing an Easter egg hunt, having a July 4th barbeque.

_____

_____

_____

_____

_____

_____

_____

_____

_____

_____

_____

_____

_____

_____

_____

_____

_____

_____

_____

_____

_____

_____

_____

What family custom would you like to pass on to your children and grandchildren?

_____

_____

_____

_____

_____

_____

_____

_____

_____

_____

What is the best holiday gift you ever gave? Received?

_____

_____

_____

_____

_____

_____

_____

_____

_____

_____

Do you share a family tradition or memory from the Fourth of July?

_____

_____

_____

_____

_____

_____

_____

_____

_____

_____

How did you celebrate Thanksgiving in your family?

_____

_____

_____

_____

_____

_____

_____

_____

_____

_____

_____

"When you look at your life, the greatest happinesses are family happinesses."

— Joyce Brothers

What is your family's favorite Christmas or Hanukkah tradition?

_____

_____

_____

_____

_____

_____

_____

_____

_____

How have any of your holiday traditions changed over the years? Have you started any new traditions?

_____

_____

_____

_____

_____

_____

_____

_____

_____

_____

_____

What were your favorite holidays? Did you have special holiday customs or foods?

_____

_____

_____

_____

_____

_____

_____

_____

_____

_____

What are your favorite family holiday memories? What are your happiest holidays?

_____

_____

_____

_____

_____

_____

_____

_____

_____

_____

_____

_____

"You don't choose your family.
They are God's gift to you, as you
are to them."

— Desmond Tutu

Can you remember any funny things that happened at holiday times? What kind of foods did your family prepare and eat during the holidays?

_____

_____

_____

_____

_____

_____

_____

_____

_____

_____

_____

Are there special holiday decorations that are part of your family's history?

_____

_____

_____

_____

_____

_____

_____

_____

_____

_____

_____

What other relatives and friends participated in your family's holiday celebration?

_____

_____

_____

_____

_____

_____

_____

_____

_____

_____

_____

Were there any unique ways that the town you grew up in celebrated the holidays as a community?

_____

_____

_____

_____

_____

_____

_____

_____

_____

_____

_____

_____

_____

What was shopping and gift-giving like in your family?

_____
_____
_____
_____
_____
_____
_____
_____

How are the holidays today different than they were years ago?

_____
_____
_____
_____
_____
_____
_____
_____
_____
_____

Are there any spiritually related memories you'd like to share?

_____
_____
_____
_____
_____
_____
_____
_____

"If the family were a fruit, it would be an orange, a circle of sections, held together but separable—each segment distinct."

—Letty Cottin Pogrebin

Foodstuffs

Each part of your home holds special memories. The kitchen is often called the heart of a home. So much time is spent there; so many important events take place there. What are some of your fondest memories that took place in your family's kitchen?

_____

_____

_____

_____

_____

_____

_____

_____

_____

Can you remember some of the most heartfelt conversations that took place in the kitchen?

_____

_____

_____

_____

_____

_____

_____

_____

_____

_____

_____

What was your favorite meal as a child? What made it your favorite meal? What were your favorite foods?

_____

_____

_____

_____

_____

_____

_____

_____

_____

_____

Did you all eat together as a family? Who did the cooking?

_____

_____

_____

_____

_____

_____

_____

_____

_____

_____

_____

Describe the typical family dinner.

_____
_____
_____
_____
_____
_____
_____
_____
_____
_____
_____

Have any recipes been passed down to you from family members?

_____
_____
_____
_____
_____
_____
_____
_____
_____
_____
_____

What has been the happiest time of your life?

_____

_____

_____

_____

_____

_____

_____

_____

_____

_____

_____

What is your happiest family memory? Describe.

_____

_____

_____

_____

_____

_____

_____

_____

_____

_____

_____

_____

What is your saddest family memory? Describe.

_____

_____

_____

_____

_____

_____

_____

_____

_____

_____

_____

_____

_____

_____

_____

_____

_____

_____

_____

_____

_____

_____

_____

Is there a family member whom you have lost and whom you are reminded of often?

_____

_____

_____

_____

_____

_____

_____

_____

_____

Do you feel that one of your elders is still with you, providing guidance? In what situations were you guided by the memory of this person, and how did it help you?

_____

_____

_____

_____

_____

_____

_____

_____

_____

_____

_____

"Things house our feelings, memories and connections with others, both living and dead. When we regard things this way, our interactions with them become spiritual exercises."

— Mary Ann Brussat

What a Gem

Is there a family heirloom that is particularly prized in your family? Describe the object. Where does it come from, and how did your family come by it?

_____

_____

_____

_____

_____

_____

_____

_____

_____

What are some of the other material heirlooms passed down in your family, such as a piece of jewelry? Who originally wore the jewelry? Why was it given? Did it mark a special occasion?

_____

_____

_____

_____

_____

_____

_____

_____

_____

_____

Heirlooms

Are there any family heirlooms that have caused disputes in you family over who got them and why? How was it resolved?

_____

_____

_____

_____

_____

_____

_____

_____

_____

_____

_____

_____

_____

_____

_____

_____

_____

_____

_____

_____

_____

_____

_____

_____

Are there any particular pieces of furniture or utensils that have been passed down in your family? What are they? Who first brought them into the family? How were they used over the generations?

_____

_____

_____

_____

_____

_____

_____

_____

_____

_____

_____

_____

_____

_____

_____

_____

_____

_____

_____

_____

_____

How did your relatives manage to hold on to these family treasures for all these years?
Was your family ever at risk of losing one of these treasures? How did they hang on to it?

_____

_____

_____

_____

_____

_____

_____

_____

_____

_____

_____

Is there a particular family treasure that was lost at some point? What was it? How did
your family react to this loss?

_____

_____

_____

_____

_____

_____

_____

_____

_____

_____

_____

_____

CHAPTER NINE

Questions and Ancestors: Tracing Your Ancestors

"How will your children know who they are if they don't know where they came from?"

— The Grapes of Wrath, John Steinbeck

Questions and Ancestors: Tracing Your Ancestors

Don't know where to start to trace your ancestors? Look in the mirror. You are the key to your genealogical past. Experts advise that the best way to start your search is to start with yourself and work backward.

The first step is to start with a generation chart—a road map to the ancestry highway placing you at the beginning and branching back one set of parents at a time. (See Chapter One, "Creating Your Family Tree.") Samples of generational charts also are available on the Internet and in genealogy books. In addition to full names, you may want to include birthdate, place of birth, date and place of marriage, date and place of death. Compiling as much of this information as possible helps in researching ancestors.

When you begin your research, it is important to know that in the United States, states and counties organize most information. There are also a number of family tree Web sites and CD-ROM packages available to help in the search. Now that public records are online, tracing your family tree is a click away.

"Genealogy: n., an account of one's descent from a man who did not particularly care to trace his own."

— Ambrose Bierce

For the Record: Sources for Family Record Information

Consider these ideas and use this space as a workbook to jot down facts that will help you in your search.

_____

_____

_____

_____

_____

_____

_____

_____

_____

_____

_____

_____

_____

_____

_____

_____

_____

_____

_____

_____

_____

_____

_____

_____

_____

_____

Church Records

Local parish churches and synagogues often have records of births, marriages, and deaths. The administrative offices of the appropriate religion may have records, such as the archives of the Diocese or Archdiocese of Catholic Churches

Do you know what church, synagogue, or house of worship they were affiliated with? Dates they may have attended?

_____

_____

_____

_____

_____

_____

_____

_____

_____

Do you have any information about baptisms/communions/bar or bat mitzvahs/marriages that might help in the search?

_____

_____

_____

_____

_____

_____

_____

_____

_____

Census Records

Census records and county records are another excellent source of information. The U.S. Census Bureau takes a national census every ten years.

Jot down the dates or a timeline showing when and where your ancestors were born to help in your search.

_____

_____

_____

_____

_____

_____

_____

_____

_____

_____

_____

_____

_____

_____

_____

_____

_____

_____

_____

_____

_____

_____

_____

Clerk's Office

Property deeds, oaths and bonds, poll and tally books, voter registration, marriage licenses, business licenses, brands, mining records, notary records and Assessor's Office tax records are all excellent sources of information.

Jot down any of these records you have or have access to before you begin your search.

_____

_____

_____

_____

_____

_____

_____

_____

_____

_____

_____

_____

_____

_____

_____

_____

_____

_____

_____

_____

_____

_____

More Sources

Military records, as well as wills and diaries, can be a valuable source of information.

What do these documents tell you about your family? Jot it down here.

_____

_____

_____

_____

_____

_____

_____

_____

_____

_____

_____

_____

_____

_____

_____

_____

_____

_____

_____

_____

_____

_____

Other Sources for Your Search

Probate Office: Case files, wills, testaments, guardianships, and adoptions;
District Court Records or Civil and Criminal Docket Books;
Naturalization Records: Declaration and Intention, Petition for Naturalization,
Certificate of Naturalization;
Land Grants and Conveyances: These records chart the distribution of land, including
records of the Surveyor General and the Court of Private Land Claims.

These records are important in that they list land grantees, heirs, family names, and relationships. Jot down access to any of these documents you have or can collect from relatives.

_____

_____

_____

_____

_____

_____

_____

_____

_____

_____

_____

_____

_____

_____

_____

_____

_____

_____

_____

_____

_____

Do you have access to private collections or published family histories? Families sometimes donate their family papers to private museum collections. In some instances, genealogists have already researched and prepared large volumes of family histories. Beginning genealogists should make it a point to consult these resources. In some cases, the work has already been done.

_____

_____

_____

_____

_____

_____

_____

_____

_____

Newspapers are an excellent source of information. Obituaries, birth, and marriage announcements, for example, provide pertinent genealogical information. Write down some of the headlines you find concerning the events occurring on the timeline of your family history.

_____

_____

_____

_____

_____

_____

_____

_____

_____

Family Photographs

Although we take photographs for granted, family photos often tell a story that is not captured anywhere else—they can document expressions, or an exact moment in time.

In handling family photos, remember that they can be damaged by too much light, extremes in temperature, extremes in humidity (either too dry or too damp), and even time. Store your photos in an area where the temperature is steady and avoid the extremes that would be found in an attic or basement.

In the digital age, we now have the opportunity to duplicate images at a minimal cost, either as a digital file or as a print made from a digital file. Old, damaged photos can also be fixed with various programs, such as Photoshop or Photo Editor.

Remember that you can have copies made in any quantity. Always have multiple copies made of your favorite family photos, and send them to relatives living in other parts of the country. Remember to write down information for your family photos so that your family members can understand the records they keep. Use the space below to take notes on some of your favorite photos and the people you might like to share them with.

To track down living relatives, the best place to search is the White Pages or the Internet. The Internet is a rich source to begin your search for ancestors, as many records are now online. There are several Web sites that are helpful; some online archives include:

www.censusfetch.com
www.ancestry.com
www.genealogy.com
www.rootsweb.com
www.ellisisland.org
www.familysearch.org
www.worldfamilies.net

Use the space below to collect other useful online resources and Web addresses.

_____

_____

_____

_____

_____

_____

_____

_____

_____

_____

_____

_____

_____

_____

_____

_____

_____

_____

"The family—that dear octopus from whose tentacles we never quite escape, nor, in our inmost hearts, ever quite wish to."

—Dodie Smith

Genealogy can be more than data. And many family historians like to create ancestor profiles that put their lives in the context of historical timelines. Items to consider including are national events such as presidential elections, military events, dates of local importance, and other historical markers. Write your historical timeline here.

Date   **Event**

Date

Event

_____

_____

_____

_____

_____

_____

_____

Date

Event

Date

Event

_____

_____

_____

_____

_____

_____

_____

Date

Event

CHAPTER TEN

The Next Generation

"The little ones leaped, and shouted, and laugh'd. And all the hills echoed."

—William Blake

The Next Generation

You have spent most of this book exploring family history and looking back at your life—the childhood memories, exciting moments, crises, and turning points. You've explored family rituals and traditions, celebrations, and special events that evoke memories tightly held in your heart. Now, it is time to look ahead and answer some of the fundamental questions that will shape your dreams and those you have for your children, their children, and the generations to come. Here are some questions to help you examine what lies ahead as you create traditions and think about hopes and dreams for the next generation.

What do you remember about the days your children were born?

_____

_____

_____

_____

_____

_____

_____

_____

_____

_____

_____

_____

What do you remember about the births of your nieces and nephews?

_____

_____

_____

_____

_____

_____

_____

_____

_____

_____

_____

The Apple and the Tree

What characteristics do your children display that remind you of yourself, your parents, an aunt or uncle, grandparents, or great-grandparents?

_____

_____

_____

_____

_____

_____

_____

_____

_____

_____

Is there a talent your children or nieces or nephews have that may have been passed down through the generations? Describe that.

_____

_____

_____

_____

_____

_____

_____

_____

_____

_____

"We all grow up with the weight of history on us. Our ancestors dwell in the attics of our brains as they do in the spiraling chains of knowledge hidden in every cell of our bodies."

— Shirley Abbott

What advice or wisdom about life that you learned from your family would you like future generations to remember?

_____

_____

_____

_____

_____

_____

_____

_____

_____

_____

What hard-earned lesson do you wish you could get your children and grandchildren to understand?

_____

_____

_____

_____

_____

_____

_____

_____

_____

_____

_____

_____

What word best describes your life? Why?

_____

_____

_____

_____

_____

_____

_____

_____

_____

_____

_____

What words best describe the lives of your children so far? Why?

_____

_____

_____

_____

_____

_____

_____

_____

_____

_____

_____

_____

"The family. We were a strange little band of characters trudging through life sharing diseases and toothpaste, coveting one another's desserts, hiding shampoo, borrowing money, locking each other out of our rooms, inflicting pain and kissing to heal it in the same instant, loving, laughing, defending, and trying to figure out the common thread that bound us all together."

— Erma Bombeck

High Hopes

What are your highest hopes for your siblings? What can you do to help make sure these hopes are realized?

_____

_____

_____

_____

_____

_____

_____

_____

_____

_____

What are your highest hopes for your children? What can you do to make sure they are realized?

_____

_____

_____

_____

_____

_____

_____

_____

_____

_____

_____

What are your dreams for your nieces and nephews? How can you help make sure those dreams come true?

_____

_____

_____

_____

_____

_____

_____

_____

_____

_____

_____

If you have grandchildren, what are your highest hopes for them? What can you do to make sure these hopes are realized?

_____

_____

_____

_____

_____

_____

_____

_____

_____

_____

_____

What do you remember about the day your grandchildren were born?

_____

_____

_____

_____

_____

_____

_____

_____

_____

_____

_____

What do you remember about the birth of your great-nieces and great-nephews?

_____

_____

_____

_____

_____

_____

_____

_____

_____

_____

_____

How do you see your children performing in their roles as parents?

_____

_____

_____

_____

_____

_____

_____

_____

_____

_____

Do you see your children using the same techniques you used with them?

_____

_____

_____

_____

_____

_____

_____

_____

_____

_____

_____

What achievements of your grandchildren are you especially proud of?

_____

_____

_____

_____

_____

_____

_____

_____

_____

_____

_____

_____

What special abilities do you see in your grandchildren? Where do they excel?

_____

_____

_____

_____

_____

_____

_____

_____

_____

_____

_____

If you have great-grandchildren, describe them. What are their names? When were they born?

_____

_____

_____

_____

_____

_____

_____

_____

_____

_____

Do you have great-great-nieces and great-great-nephews?

_____

_____

_____

_____

_____

_____

_____

_____

_____

_____

_____

Which family characteristics do you see in your grandchildren and great-nieces and great-nephews?

_____

_____

_____

_____

_____

_____

_____

_____

_____

_____

Have your children or grandchildren grown up? If not, how do you imagine the future for them? If they are grown up, has the future you imagined for them come true? How is it the same? How is it different?

_____

_____

_____

_____

_____

_____

_____

_____

_____

_____

"*A baby is God's opinion that life should go on.*"

—Carl Sandburg

Dream Makers

Are there dreams of your own that you would like to realize? What are you doing to make those happen?

_____

_____

_____

_____

_____

_____

_____

_____

_____

_____

If you have a spouse or significant other, what dreams do you hope may come true for your loved one? What can you do to help make this happen?

_____

_____

_____

_____

_____

_____

_____

_____

_____

_____

_____

What has been your proudest moment as a parent?

_____

_____

_____

_____

_____

_____

_____

_____

_____

_____

Of all the things you learned from your parents, what is the one thing you hope you have passed on to your children?

_____

_____

_____

_____

_____

_____

_____

_____

_____

_____

_____

_____

What would you like to see happen in the next 10 years?

_____

_____

_____

_____

_____

_____

_____

_____

_____

_____

What would you like to see happen in the next 20 years?

_____

_____

_____

_____

_____

_____

_____

_____

_____

_____

_____

_____

"We are the children of many sires, and every drop of blood in us in its turn . . . betrays its ancestor."

— Ralph Waldo Emerson

Back to the Future

Through this book you've retraced many steps, taken many backward glances, and asked your relatives to also remember as far back to the beginning as their memories can stretch. The result is this precious collection of family stories, traditions, and bonds of love and blood. You have created a lens for family members to look back and ahead, to your shared heritage and what is yet to come. You've also created a bridge for your children and the next generations to take those values, fun family quirks, pastimes, and rituals, and carry the meaning of those stories into the future. Family is forever, and now you have a book that reminds those you love the most about the ties that bind.

_____

_____

_____

_____

_____

_____

_____

_____

_____

_____

_____

_____

_____

_____

_____

_____

_____

_____

_____

_____

_____

_____

_____